MW01234341

# THE CARNIVAL OF AFFECTION

## PHILIP F. CLARK

**SIBLING RIVALRY PRESS**
LITTLE ROCK, ARKANSAS

*DISTURB / ENRAPTURE*

Sibling Rivalry Press, LLC
PO Box 26147
Little Rock, AR 72221

info@siblingrivalrypress.com

www.siblingrivalrypress.com

ISBN: 978-1-943977-41-3

Library of Congress Number: 2017944195

This title is housed permanently in the Rare Books and Special
Collections Vault of the Library of Congress.

First Sibling Rivalry Press Edition, November 2017

*For my sister, Kathleen M. Clark*

# TABLE OF CONTENTS

*I am an orphan of fire....*

*In the quiet dark,*

*fathers*

*reappear.*

# A SÉANCE IN THE DOLLHOUSE

"Let's look," you said,
    pointing softly, one by one
to each room with your index finger:
    the bedroom, the bright
kitchen, the dark stairs; your thumb on me
    as if I were a globe,
and you had to find my latitude.
    You said, "See there, see, there?"
    The house of your hands on me.

The little table, the quiet chair; tiny cups. The dolls
    won't tell. Nothing breaks here
    behind the door. The poor clock stopped. I saw
    outside, over there. "Outside? No," you said,
    "in here."

Every time you touched me I
    would join the toys;
it was easy getting there, getting out
and going in. The door would always
    open then.
    With every touch you mapped on me,
I'd walk from room to room; each a box
    of noise on my long, slow walks to the not-touching room.

# THE READERS

(AFTER ROBERT HAYDEN)

I still hear him turning pages. Every morning I would wake to that sound in the dark blue hour. The time in the mornings, so brief for him, before I became his work instead of all the work he still had to do. As I dressed in the cold, I would hear him preparing our food: hear the butter skate the grill and the old bread. With sleep still on me, I would come into the room and see him working slowly, with no urgency, except to make things last before I left for school. He would quietly place our cups on the table in the adamantly warming room. Our eyes would seldom meet; they never needed to. We had glanced at those mirrors before. The house had more to say than we did; it hissed with its winds and split its linoleum underfoot. My father and I would eat, his interrupted book there on the table. What book was he reading this time? And where was he in it, when I interrupted his dream? How long does it take to read a book when you have a son?

# JOE

He wore his fire; half beauty, half beast. His face the deal
breaker every night in the bar, no matter how charming they found
him. He grew used to the averted eyes for years.

He settled into unsettling everyone. He was the wallpaper and the fly,
drinking up and taking everything in with his one good eye.
The other, a dare of blue glass.

There were things before the fire. Before is a whole space now, a book
he can read. A fire. He thinks of what it felt like. Now he knows
how to quiet fires, to listen for licks of flame. A kind of living moves him.

He remembers skin, before it was something else. The body burns
quickly. That vagrant stare of mouths. He knew the sound
of eyes on skin.

Books never failed him. The warmth of ink and the light
inside his head. One eye could still cry, and did. But a book is not a hand
or a chest on which to lie.

He loved the sound and feel of pages; the hand of books. That skin.
Someone looks at him, says hello with an outstretched smile.
The want of words was the problem now.

His mouth with its empty cavern voices softly dimmed. A cab together
and then bed. He had never undressed with a man's eyes on him.
He stood, faltered and turned his eye away.

The man reached to him,
and touched Joe's skin. Shaking, burning,
all night the man became a book.

# LACRIMOSA

Where I grew up, wakes were a sparring ground—
furor was the only defense to grief. Someone
had to fight the rant and terror of all those flowers.

That is how I remember the dead,
lone among loud voices and the odor
of calla lilies and plastic chairs—caves
where a child could seek solace
from black-veiled, arguing aunts.

I played solitaire with the prayer cards,
until I was slapped soundly by a velvet glove.

I waited for the priest to arrive.
He was beautiful; I remember his cassock
whispering toward me.
Everyone was quiet then. I remember that.

As all of us stood, I cried;
not for the lonely dead—for the living—
who dread the sumptuous air,
the unadorned smile, the fervent prayer.

# THE FATHERS

I steadied you in the bathroom as you pissed,
drunk and shaking. I was the only one who
would make sure you didn't fall.
You kept talking about the friends you lost
in the war.

One morning, you took me to school in the cold.
I was seven. "Hold my hand," you said, but even then
I could tell it made you feel strange. Now I am
holding hands all over the place, and every other
flesh I can hold on to. Your hand turned pages.

When I was ten, you took me to watch
the boxing matches. I hated the smoke
and punches and sweat. I asked to leave.
The other fathers knowingly
nodded as you walked me out of the room.

That night you simply read your paper.
You smoked. I went to bed, listening for you,
but only heard punch after punch.

Years later, I held you again in the hospital,
walking in silence down the long hall; eyes
watching our slow progress
toward the latrine. I can still smell the ammonia.
Then you were gone.
You dropped dead in the street, while I
was home choosing a tie, or maybe I was
reading, or trying to call you. After all,
it had been years.

You read to me on mornings when I could
not sleep. Your voice was all I needed.
Now I write words you'll never read.
I still have that book of yours, with a cracked
spine. I lift it and turn its pages in my hands.
I hold your voice. I open myself.

# EXCAVATION

We unearth the other bodies, having buried our own.
We contemplate bone, buttock and lip; the rise
of the back into the neck, the slope of the glute,
the dark slide of the tongue.
Inveterate archaeologists of the kiss,
we compare his thighs to this, your calf
to the one in the moonlight that night on the beach.
In the dust it all seems clear. The bodies intertwine—
dolls made from many doll parts; this one, a beautiful eye
battered blue, the muscled arm potent with veins,
the fine chest and nipple now licked and slept upon
to be remembered in some distant summer:
Oh yes, oh yes, I had him.

*You enter me with spotless grammar.*

*What I love the most is the instant just before I touch*


*You—*


*Before flesh feels what the eye has longed for.*

# MITCH

The small town wakes up slowly as he watches its lights come on;
the voyeur who loves his job. He sips his coffee, semi-hard.

He knows more about the neighbors in the dark
than they do of him in the day. He feels the cold on his skin

through the parted curtain,
the ice of deeper angers in darker rooms.

His partner in their bedroom sleeps soundly, he never hears
a step, or the break on the stair. And Zeke, fat old thing,

knows this quiet ceremony too well to growl or lift his head.
The bed seems years away, but Mitch eases back inside

the still warm skin. No hand returns a touch.
He lies awake and listens for the clues: John McKay has

started his car; his wife puts the milk bottles on the steps.
Jim Simon calls "good morning," as he reaches

for the daily news; a muttered reply leaves nothing mended.
Frances Jones has slammed her door again, the constant rebuke.

He thinks of her son, the boy who drowned last summer,
in an instant—or so it seemed. We forgot to keep watch.

And then suddenly everyone was looking around and screaming.
That thin body. He thought the boy looked content, dripping there beside

his mother screaming, at everything and nothing. At nothing, and the air.
The sad work done, we walked home, beaten and sun-burned.

Mitch remembers a certain touch at a certain hour,
a certain light; just like these mornings—which devour

thoughts, unpacked plans, second chances and last remains.
Sleep soon wrestles him. He does not feel his partner rise

as he leaves the bed, nor can he see the look on Tom's still-tired
eyes as he looks in the mirror. Most of their days are like this.

They meet, eat silently together. They murmur
the news of the day and its dead.

Oh, the sleep that pardons.

# LEARNING

*Put up your fists*,
my father said.
And so I did.
So I have been
ever since;
I've won
nothing, gained less.
Blood weary, well-worn,
I resist what I can.
Father, did you think
I would learn
that the heart,
with an uppercut,
had fists in return?
The swarm cheers
the down-turned thumb.
*Be a man*, he said.
And so I've tried.
*Fight like a man*, he said.
I've loved men like a man
instead.

# THE DAY I BECAME A PAPI CHULO

It was my usual walk from work,
in suit and tie, tired from the day.
I approached the ball park. They came
toward me, laughing—a gang of about five
energized, jeering, laughing young men—
still dressed in their baseball stripes, bats and gloves
in hand, smiles still wide from an obvious win.
As they rushed past, an arm glanced mine and
I heard the words, "Hermoso papi chulo!"
From what little Spanish I knew,
it was a compliment.
(But one is never sure.)
And thus crowned, I turned to them,
smiled, embarrassed, red.
They spoke other words in Spanish I could
not catch, and the young man then said
"Mister, do you understand?"
I nodded. I wanted to say something back,
but I didn't know, or have, the words with
which to crown them in return.

# THE BEGGAR'S WELCOME

He stopped and asked if I could spare some change.
I thought, Oh yes, I could spare so much: another job,
a new home, other clothes, better weather, more chances,
less pain. Yes, I could spare some change.
He held out his hand—callused, sooted, cracked.
I groped for my wallet, and I held his eyes:
still young, if half alive; as if they and his body were not
the same—there were the chances he mistook,
the changes on a dime—the house, the car, the wife
or lover, the constantly put off grave.
All I had was a clean last twenty.
Without a thought, I handed it to him.
As he gently took it, his hand in mine, I knew:
It's all we ever want—the holding. The asking
is never as hard as the needing, the accepting
never as hard as the taking.

## AT THE BAR

"Paul said you didn't mind
when Darren didn't come
because John had unexpected guests
and Eric didn't have a car that night
when Ken thought the party
began at eight and so had a conflict
with an opera at the Met and Andrew tried
to get a date last minute but ran
into Mark at Boxers on the way
and they sped off for a kissing spell
before Alex could even tip the bartender
who Parker had seen last week with
Jim at the Cloisters but looked away
and didn't want to be seen by the
guy he was with who he recognized
as Tim who had brushed him off
last week at G's when Scott gave
a party there for Allen who was so
drunk by then that Marcus
split early after two gins comped
once again by George who was already
going bankrupt before Thomas
said, 'Whoa boy, let's go. It's late
and no one here is really interesting anyway. . .'

## HANDS

In the dream I woke up hearing two voices:
my father and I were speaking—
I had grown older and he with me,
rather than the way it turned out. As I rose
from the bed, it was empty and ice clear.
But he was there, talking—a cold breath—turning to me,
holding something like fire, and his touch—
     I keep touching,
     I keep touching
as if my hands being touched could become
fire too. *Remember what I said*, and then he was gone.

The conversation died.

I wanted to speak, but I had no tongue,
no touch, no fire. I wake up
some mornings
     touching,
     touching,
pressing my hands to the voice in the bed.
I rise beside him reaching,
the tongue of my hands in my head.
     *I will.*
     *I will.*

You, ferryman, what land is this?

*It is your future.*

Then we cannot stop here now.

*It has come early. Disembark.*

I will not leave the boat.

*The sea has left you.*

# THE CORRESPONDENCE

He enters you not against
your will, but against your desire;
fumblings for purchase,
hands and legs trying to
find a position of accommodation—
works like a kiss but there are no
lips to hold on to. You think
you'll get through an hour of this
because something inside
needs it—just not this.
You try to find something
on his face to land on, some
tear or sweat that might initiate welcome.
What you wouldn't give for a right
hand or the wrong mouth.
You start writing a letter in your head,
to some old lover. You stop writing,
and he comes.

## TO A DIVER

The measured, slow climb.
You stand, a seer

poised at the top of your heaven.
The wind is kissing you dry.

Far below, I sense your concentration:
your eyes on other horizons. Your body

sure, intent. A split second of choice and lurch;
a twist, a line, a circle as you soar down.

You stop my breath
as your beauty perfects

an exclamation point.
Your soul an ampersand.

# THE SEXTANT

The shape of what we sought
took a strange turn: It was this,
the soft giving in, not the

metal and cut of it, not the wet brine
or the slow and long grasp I had
planned for. It was silence we came to,

watching our bodies become the years
away, the skin and marble-hard sea
of desire and its premonition.

Those arm-on-the-back farewells
set now like clocks inside us. Naked
and close, I was hope, and

you were consolation,
as day after day you
remained a grief in my throat.

Sated with waiting we drifted here, itinerant,
not lost but unable to land. And then we did.
We prayed for a bit. Not often.

Touch became the sea of us;
boated in bed, I held you and waited,
for the end of something still ahead.

# THE DANCES

The soup was sometimes sparse; not
the making of it, not the leavening
of our house with the oven's gradual fire.

Eating was done mostly in silence;
not for a lack of words but for the
grateful sound of mouths being fed.

Days were not always filled with
many things to do, so we filled them
with things we imagined.

She often sat with her thoughts,
our mother—and given time she would
begin to tell us things. We'd wait

and patiently listen for those
incandescent secrets she would
pepper in: The sister who ran away,

the brother-in-law who shot his
wife, the child from another marriage.
Those parsed bits of the family tree

strewn across years. We were grateful;
we grew and were soon telling our own.
"One time," she'd say—and our

eyes would light up. Neighbors
were kind, knowing our common
griefs. They had attended all of them.

She used to dance quite a bit,
it was said, and I faintly remember
a dress she wore, and black heels.

"Your father was slow," she laughed.
"I was always leading." So we could
see them both there, on the ballroom

floor—my mother spinning, my
father trying to get out of the way.
The dresses, the colors, the lights,

men in ties sweating to their waists,
music like a gambit in the night, starting
the next hour, and the next,

when, quiet and one by one, the dancers left
the floor, and rooms would warm in other years.

## ROSES

I arrived just as they
were making your bed. I thought,
"They've moved him," but no,
you were dead. Someone else
was moving in. Your sisters had just left.
As the attendant finished cleaning up
I was about to turn away. I noticed
on the table, a Red Rose tea bag—
and I smiled. Your friend Jim would
always send you a box of them,
and on each tag, like an advent calendar's
windows, he'd pasted porn under each rose.
Your laugh used to startle the nurses. As I held one
small rose, I was going to stay in the room and ask
questions. But I dropped the relic. It was not
a room for the past.
I went home and made my bed. I lay
there thinking of you—of just having missed you,
the few minutes I might have saved
had I rushed, or taken the train.
I began to laugh, hearing in my head your words,
"Oh Darling, look at these!"
I rose from my bed. I looked at my life. I took my meds.

# INTERIM

Time is of the essence you said with your open arms,
standing in the breeze and salt, watching the waves.

But these months have garnered their opulence
of memory, their vast ability to flounce retrospect.

My body is an array of your shadows and touches
like some new cashmere that softens regret.

The length of longing disperses our old rebuke
and the clamor of its armor.

Nothing remarkable in this, that I love you, or
something to that effect. More is seen than spoken.

I can neither look ahead nor see behind me
without some beauty fastening itself to this now.

There is something to be said for persistence,
its fallow jaunts through my time and days.

Nothing changes; the moon arcs its mindful
lemon eye and sets my faltering clock inside.

*I never took your body for granted;*
*now, as it is constantly missed, it at times appears*

*at rest in the room, sun-muscled*
*and warm—configured by my stray illumined thoughts*

*of how a body pleases in the dark*
*where absence has its harbor.*

# VINCENT

Impeccably dressed, he put a last rub of scent on his carotid artery
knowing full well that will make it last all day. The brisk note of
lemon wafts in the hall as he locks the door and says good morning
to the neighbor. She nods, as always, never says a word.
He takes the stairs. His new shoes don't make a sound; the best leather, they
feel like he's worn them for years. Not a hair out of place,

freshly combed and shaved, he walks into the bright sun.
The park is green, the taxi yellow, the sky is blue. The light is red.
People stare up at him, three inches at least above their heads.
Almond-eyed, he's lost in thought, and contemplates the day.
He walks ahead, pink-faced with purpose—a slight smile shows his perfect teeth.

A man turns to stare, and turns again. Other men do. Women stop.
As he passes by them like some private benediction, some holy "Yes" quietly
whispered only to them, their faces change for a moment and take on an air
of concupiscence, parting glances, the secret that will last the day.
He knows full well what he does to them. What can he say or
do? They catch their breath and he catches his cab.
The city spins past and he thinks he will travel to Ireland again

or to Spain, or France. He'll walk in Timbuktu. There is time of course,
for these things. For now he tips his fare generously, as he always does
and proceeds to walk into his glass and silver tower.
He reminds himself to send some flowers home to his apartment
before he arrives back at the end of the day. He squanders no time, walks away

# THE CARNIVAL OF AFFECTION

Invent my body with me; surely we have time
     to render flesh and bone.

     Be my Adam for a while.

Place my smile, awkward; place my eyes, hopeful;
     help my mouth learn its place to kiss.

Embrace this arm, empty, and its brother,
     empty too. Stitch a new heart inside.

     Touch where Thomas doubted.

Wind these legs around you; they are air,
     and I cannot steal away.

What we fear is only love; what we make
     of it is here: invent with me

my body, love, render me a kiss of bone.
     Abrade my flesh with wonder.

# BODY, TENDER THIEF

Body, tender thief—
    you pick among us,
sure in your magpie choices.

Your stolen goods are skin, hair,
    muscle and memory,
pawned and haggled over time.

Calmly in your taking,
    we lose a thought here,
there—a tooth or eye.

Itinerant, industrious, you cleave
    first one breath, then two.
Quietly you stop the heart.

You barter all desire,
    proud to own its end.
Patient, ardent, you win.

# THE MINOTAUR

They sent me away. Terror is my food. I eat with one eye open.
My mouth never rests. It shows signs of struggle.
See how the birds land on my horns night and day,
mooned and sunned by desire and thirst.
I speak and nothing is born on my tongue.
The flowers die in my hand.

Hate fosters strange children here who look at me and ask,
"When can we go home?" They stroke my face and think
I can speak, but my mouth is bone, my jaw weary from questions.
The children consider that I might live. There are no doctors for this.
I have checked every day.

I have tried to sew my eyes shut,
but vision is the constant dog looking up to be stroked.
My cloth is a stone shirt; my hooves cry when I walk.
I watch the homeless gather their bottles and cans.
With hope, I write my name with my tongue.
No one deciphers my runes; strange grasses settle in my heart.

A town closed itself to me as I begged at the gates
for a place to sleep. "We have no beds here," they said.
"Step away, you are dreaming, turn back." I carry my
cloven loam of last good will and try to plant it.
No earth will take me. I would better eat fire
and be watched by the stars.

Only you stopped for me and took my face in your hands.
Finding my skin flayed, you searched for water
to wash me. You covered me with brine, salted
my wounds to wake me. "Do you know where you are?"
I watched the blood on my hands turn to ash
and could not answer. A child wept and kissed me.

"Do you see what you've done?" She pointed her hand
behind me and I saw the path I had traveled begin to sink. The trees
smelled of pine and tar. A porphyry moon rose in the East
and three women lifted baskets of stars, spilling light
onto my feet. They kissed me.
"You have far to go," they said. They gave me a crown.

I took the clocks apart until the cave was strewn with Time.
The walls wept; someone called to me.
I had to eat again. I walked to the edge of the world
and asked, "When will this be over?" They cried out,
"He is here! He is here!" Night seeped
lower and I cowered for sleep. It did not come.

Black as a changling swan, I tied my belt around my neck
and I looked for a place to hang. The woods had given
up their branches long ago, cut for fire. I have to sew some
way to live. Hoof forward, hoof forward, the ground soon rose
below me. I ate the dank air and the brindled light.
I am the Once-Man, sad in his maze, looking for someone.

## JAMES

He is immersed
in his unguents and scents: his
freshly-washed hair and soaped hands;
the stiff starch of his bright white lace
surplice and alb, smelling of the air.
His polished shoes glisten, and his perfect
fingernails—as he prepares the wine,
and steadies the Verger's staff.
The sun on his eyes even has
the odor of sanctity; the herbs
in the vestry quicken with aroma.
He moves slowly in his tasks,
his vestments whispering, as
he feels his body underneath
his robes; and he blesses himself
and feels the metal cock ring there.

# A FRACAS IN THE MEMORY PALACE

It happened that morning, when
you forgot whether to butter the bread
or comb your hair. You combed
the butter, then your head. I walked in.

I heard you among the crowd of objects—
table, cup, saucer, cake.
You thought the cake was a hat.
The cup was ice cream.

You kept combing.
I sat you down, took your hand;
gentled, kissed and unworded you.
I combed your hair.

*With nothing to give,*

*we sat in your monk-spare room.*

*The moon rode the window,*

*the table was laid with promise.*

*You fed me cold beer, old bread*

*and possibility. We were naked,*

*afraid and glad.*

# MISS HAVISHAM'S FIRE

Miss Havisham went up in an ardent orange
flame—a gladiolus that bloomed fast and thick—

catching her breath somewhere between
ecstasy and surprise. The table soon flowered too.
Everything bloomed: the silk

and the chair; her lace and desire.

The windows flared as she turned,
looking around at the fiery room whose

furniture for years
was only you.

# BARDO

They say I died in my sleep.
They murmur in the room, reaching
for the books on my shelf.
"He was so well-read."
I tap them on the shoulder—
"No! Turn around, I'm here!"
An old lover speaks of my habit
for vocabulary, picking out a book
he once gave me.

"This was a birthday gift, on a day
we fought. You didn't want to get him angry."
You smiled, and I tapped you again.
"I'm here! Just look, turn around!"
I walked with them through all my rooms.
They commented on my taste in clothes.
I wrapped my arms around each of them,
ran my hands over their faces and kissed
their lips. "Why are they dreaming?"

# A PAVANE FOR SIX FLOORS

So this was the dying: not the prayers,
not the hand-holding or the keeping of watch.
It was this black sea inside your mouth.

As we stared, you slowly filled with the dark wine
that you officially drowned in. We heard
ourselves making the necessary calls.

They walked up the stairs with a dark red body bag.
Two suited old men, taking their time, stopping to catch their breath.
We passed an ironic smile between us.

So this was death—the folding, pulling, moving of you—
from bed to floor, from floor to door. At the top of the stairs
with a weary look down, like Orpheus in love, the morticians

began to descend, step by marble step. At each landing a door
would open, curious eyes peered out. What a procession dear sister,
with us bringing up the rear—a pavane for six floors.

We almost waved goodbye at the hearse
but caught ourselves—looked at each other, lost at whether
to laugh or cry. So this was death: rapidly closing doors,

thick autumn air and a shortness of breath. With no voice
to speak with, we chewed on silence like warm bread
Upstairs in your room, we gathered up the sheets, the pillows,
empty cups, a half-filled bottle of urine. A new needle.
The night drew on. We thought of more things to do. We never
said a word, enjoying this last busy work. Still attending to you.

# THE HANGMAN'S POOR GIFT

The hangman's poor gift
was this: soft hands on their last
day—a mean comfort paid with years

of placing the rope just so; of settling
the hood with care—quieting the
loud world for once, and the
shaking lips. When he

held the knot and then let go,
he stood back in the dark—
its only sentry.

# THE RUNE

The boy was making something.
They were at the beach near the edge of the water,
The father reached for his son's hand; the man's
fingers curling—calloused and loamed
with work as they curved toward his son.
Crowds walked along the dune.
The sun glinted in the boy's eyes.
As he held his hand, the father looked down
at what the boy had made: some fingered
rune, incising the sand with a secret.
The boy smiled up at him, "You don't know
what it says," and he reached for him,
in a language the father would know
and the water not wash away.

# ADAM

You strode up from the subway's sooty flux
into the cold, precise December air—an obvious prince
of the haberdashers.

Navy melton, grey flannel, and a certain cashmere;
shoes shining like freshly-made caramel, silk scarf
adroitly placed—a bright outrageous shout

among the dim wormy beiges.
Your creases razored bows through the surge
of admiring glances. Your face

perfectly rosed, square chin shaved to an inch of its life,
hair gelatined to tines. Your shirt an Antarctic white.
Your tie —a gladsome green.

Was it only I who spied the inching thread,
undone by your stride, the spreading stammer
in your side? As you passed me, your cologne almost wept.

*Lazarus sleeps his dark*
*whispered dreaming. We, sad sentinels*

*and sirens, call—*
*urging him back.*

*He feels our longing; taking*
*a breath, his mouth begins*

*its waking.*

## LOUIS BELFAST

I met him in a Dublin bar,
his bright white hair shining
like some last call light.
I pushed among the crowd
and stood behind him, my eyes
trying to catch the bartender's
tattooed glance.

As luck would have it, I got
a seat next to him, once its
previous owner stumbled to the door.
With a sidelong glance, we nodded.
I tried to order a drink. He asked,
"American?"
"New Yorker, yes."
"Louis, Belfast," and I thought
at first it was his full name.

He turned ice blue eyes to the bar.
"A Guinness, Declan, when you have a chance."
When it came he placed it in front of me.
"They're slow here, this time of night. Cheers."
He was maybe in his 70's; a strong broad
chest, well-dressed, smoothed-faced.
A blackened thumb tapped a beat to
Crowded House, drumming in the room.

He leaned into me; in a clipped and
beautiful brogue, he said,
"They say we have the gift of gab
so be prepared, I probably won't shut up."
He'd traveled, taught, had a former wife
in a former life. His lover died.

"I'm monkish now, all I love
to do is read." For the rest of the night,
Guinness after Guinness (I learned the art
of the round) we spoke of Joyce, and James,
Dickinson, Manley Hopkins, Bowen.
I don't remember getting outside the bar.
"Will you come back to us, here in Dublin?
You must take my number down."

He hailed a cab. His strong arm settled
me in; he leaned into the window for a kiss.
"Get home safe, lad. You know, there really is
a death of the heart." Louis Belfast strode away.

# THE SECRET LIFE

The second home in Cap Ferrat;
the boyfriend and the wife;
the flat in London,
the ambassadorship in Spain; one
bank account in Montreal, one bank
account in France; the Picasso that
he pondered, won at the highest price.
The bespoke suits and the baseball cap,
the way he learned Walloon; his penchant
for the opera; his acumen for fame.
The silver urn of ashes inscribed
with his unknown name.

# MENELAUS SUPPORTING PATROCLUS

He grips his soldier
and stares, aghast

at the road ahead.
The breath and the weight are heavy.

Foot stumbles to foot; he sweats.
The body, naked, uncoils in his grasp.

He tightens his arm around
the flesh, feels the musculature

and smells the sweat.
He carries, he carries, he steps.

Foot to foot and to future
he pushes against air

and breath. Waist to chest
he holds, he holds,

he remembers, he touches,
he lifts and kisses the mouth.

Flesh to flesh the carrier
trembles, falters. The warriors gone,

the spoils of war over, there is only
breath. Foot to foot, he bears the flesh.

He listens, he looks, he looks.
The body stiffens.

# GONE

On the train in the morning
in a crunch of bodies and sweat
I read the news: ". . . have successfully
'deleted' the virus from the body." Gone.

Gone—all those years
of oh I wish you would leave me
oh please leave me, please go.
Gone. Eloped to Las Vegas perhaps.

Erased. Like chalk across my body,
a fine powder of forgetfulness,
with just a few swipes—all those names
and faces. Gone. The letters burned.

It left my body. No long good-byes,
no rent overdue. No thank-yous.
I looked at myself, and waited
for the change to begin—the skin

to soften once again, the face to fill,
the hair to glow, the eyes to shine.
Gone. The years, all gone. What magic!
All the pretty pills I used to play chess with:
the blue King, the pink Queen,
the red and white Rook.
Gone. It took everything with it.
Except these: humor, anger and memory;
a certain truth told slant, like the poet said.

Obliterated. With a needle no less.
"Zero balance due." Gone, like last night's
misbegotten moon. Now, out of work,
the pallbearer's hands have nothing to do.

# THE MODEL

### (AFTER JOHN DEAKINS'S PHOTOGRAPH OF GEORGE DYER)

The body is the detritus, flesh gone
soft, the muscled skin obedient to
its final hours; the chest slack, the face a portent.
He sits, a leg crossed, the foot relaxed, unshod.
The hair, dark and oiled.
Even the room is pensive: paint and brushes
the furniture of claustrophobic doom.
He thinks he'll get through this.
The skin has been loved to no avail.
It is the world of the back of things,
a canvas facing away; its bone of wood
a prescient grasp for purchase.
The light in the room is from above,
some last benediction—a call to waking,
and questions. Suited, he is beautiful,
strong and the center of attention.
The morning is flaccid and filled with augury.
The edges have ripped the skin—a scar
suffused with some memory of pain.
This is the world of an urgent art,
the room silent, except for the constant
sound of the camera. He is hungry,
perhaps needs drink. He is about to turn
and face us, show us it is not really like this.

# MARTIN

Martin was known for a magnificent chest.
We waited all winter for the spring, when, like some
first bird announcing a change in the weather,
he would slowly disrobe from his shirt.

Those arms would twist over his head,
tousling his deep red hair, and the stomach
with its six-pack would flatten us too.

The surge of his skin, from nipple
to nipple, would stop our conversation.
He'd sit or stand, as if this was common
to see: in the street walking by, such a man.

His back perfect from swimming, Martin
moved like Hadrian come to life; his laugh
and glutes the perfect foil for our stricken eyes
suddenly poised on such beauty.

And that would be it for the hot day, his
meander up and down the damp streets, as he
and friends spoke of last night's opera, pizza
or an exhibition—the de Koonings at the Met.

It was fun, he and we knew, this public
display—there before us, strangers or friend,
to wonder how in the world such a man
was made from such ardent hands.
"Can you imagine," some would say,
and imagine we would the feel of him, the way
a lucky midnight partner might be given
the chance to sweat there.

One summer, late August and wet—
the city humming and almost empty—
Martin strode out of a bar. A strange look
in his eye warned, striking us with its glass.

"We all get old," someone said as
Martin stopped and asked for a light,
blew out one breath, and, smelling of
vetiver, he killed us again.

I am an orphan of fire and
a seer eye; a rank coil
of panic rummaging
in a satchel of curses
and curiosity.

I break your flesh
and make music
on the harp of your bones.
To love me requires
an avid mouth.
Longing is the air I eat.

# THE SEER

The lank dark oils the bed
like a scarifying needle, blood-
tipped, red and ready for work
on your dreams. You whisper

the secrets of men and past
lives: the lover, the husband,
trickster, gangster, priest.

I move closer and proffer
an ardent ear—thinking that
I might appear. The light
in the room is a knell, a kiss,
on this audience of two.

My hand is mute to touch
where skin has become a veil.
The strange bones of language
wander the room.

# THE BOOT

Omen of the foot.
Black, weathered,
slick with a snake-tongued step,
the calf's leathered matador.
Heel, buckle-belled, silver-edged
finger grope, one slow toe tap
urges 'Come here.' I bend to
the hand's companion, my lip's acolyte,
a crotch-heavy press of 'Yes.'

# ICARUS CONSIDERS

Aloft upon the air of his hubris, Icarus
lifts his waxen hope. His father's
gloaming, worried eye watches
from the sun-lanced chariot, where
the horses strain and step,
nervous with doom.
Icarus invites the air
and slowly rises, naked, feeling
the heat glowing in
the orb—up, up, up—
eyes filled with the flame
in front of him, he
glances to the forgotten
world below, where
he was once tethered, taut,
and caged in a cold shallow
skin. His body begins to glisten
as he rises—up, up, up—
the pearled wax an arrow straight
along his spine. He rises, he rises,
with ease. The sun reaches his face
and names him.
At once he is no longer a body,
but its cauldron.
He hears a sound. There is a pull
on his shoulders; a strange weight begins.
He turns and reaches. The wax, the wax!
One shoulder candles, and then the other.
Icarus considers—
he tries to pull up, to no avail of curses.
The air has said, "No," and he
begins to vault down to the world
again. His arms and body, sore with the

weight of wax, the lie of it,
strain him. He cries out as his eyes
darken. Swift, swift, he falls
—down, down, down—
the air hot with his speed, he
writhes, caught in the golden straps
now a surplice of descent; a cloak
made of lost promise. He hears the horses,
and his father's voice.
The land comes up to hold him,
the wax now cold, a casket wound
around him. He listens with one
last breath, and sees the world go green;
he feels the lambent air touch
his length. Icarus considers the air,
and is done.

# THE DRONE

The vindictive screech seeps from televisions,
millions of them like bright eyes in a dark wood. A child
works on an old computer, struggling with his common core.
A mother makes a bed, prepares her grief. A father
has yet to find a job. The bar closes; one lone hanger-on
wonders if he has enough for a tip.

Someone is beheaded. A woman begs for change.
A fine party is underway, with porcelain and crystal
and the whispers of the rich—their clothes a sound
like no other—that sibilant silk and cashmere.

A pilot watches the moon, with his cargo
full of souls, dreaming of the stars.
A document is signed and lives disappear—
it's easy, it's ink. Kids hang out on a corner, smoking,
drinking; they learn that there is still that line
called 'it ends here.' They go silent at a flashing light.

Two girls discuss a breakup text, going over it again
for clues, like a tarot of bones that would tell them why
it happened. Someone laughs at the news.
"He's at least telling the truth," they say. But the truth
is somewhere else, in some other room or country,
some onyx forest where the animals leave illegible scat.
The drone is here at home. It has its audience of takers.
Dice are thrown in vast casinos; the price of pills rises;
a body bag is quietly lifted down a flight of stairs.
In silent hospital rooms, a few souls are awake,
tied to their blood and tubes. The nurses play cards.
The doctors sleep. A clock has stopped at half past nine.
The city lights up or the farm goes dark.

Someone goes to bed loving some small thing: a child
or an old photograph of one. The office buildings rise,
and the subways swell up with itinerant workers.
Heads are bowed these days, but with other things.
A continent away, it is a day ahead and someone
goes to sleep the day before. "I just missed you,"
someone says, "by seconds."

A man reads late into the night, having lowered
the rant and the noise. But he can't really stop
hearing it: those mouths that keep going like that Beckett
play, buried up to their lips—nothing left but language,
or its grunt. He turns in bed and reaches
for a body, like the blind to braille.

# MULBERRY STREET

My mother was dreaming. She was young,
skating on Mulberry Street. Suddenly tall bales
of cotton, just off the ships, started to fall on her.
She was buried and trying to claw a way out,
frightened, but her skates were now huge
and weighed her down. She ripped and ripped
at the bales, trying to push them off. Slowly
my father awakened her, "Stella, Stella, wake up—
you're dreaming; you're tearing my shirt."

In all these years gone, I remember my mother's
dream and I like to think that my father held her
that night in their rooms in some address I never knew,
both of them listening to the many other voices
still up, still poor and awake in the street's cooler tenancies,
on that night near Chinatown, where they might
have perhaps gone for dinner before going home
to the heat of the two rooms they could hardly afford.

None of us were born yet. I look at old pictures of
Mulberry Street and I wonder where it was that
my mother skated; where the stevedores
piled the bales of new cotton she was buried in,
leaving my father to wake her and save her
there on Mulberry Street where the sound and smell
of horses could still be heard, and the few cars too.
The cool waft of river not far away in hot summer
would lift and cower over the tenements
and my mother would dream of some place wide open,
and my father would never sleep. My mother, dreaming
on Mulberry Street.

# A WALK ON FERRY BEACH, MAINE

What a December—with its hot surprise!
The stretch of beach alive with a fat sun, like an eye,
as we strolled, dogs running to the water's edge—
feeling that same strange change of time.

The dune grasses green as we stretched there,
and the water shone like white glass bones.
Trees spotted with deep red berries gleamed
as we, astonished, strode by their electric kingdoms.

Brine-crackled birds rushed over the moorings;
the air was filled with the hope of the
hesitant, not sure of its sudden new heat.
We sat, watched and simply lifted our faces.

What else could one do but give thanks? You laughed,
and I turned to you, at some joke we shared and I saw
winter ease its hand, filling you with a grace
of something close to the sun you were dressed in.

## PUBLICATION CREDITS

"The Readers," "Learning," and "Lacrimosa" were published on The Good Men Project. 2015. "Learning" was also published in *Assaracus*, Vol. 2. 2010.

"At the Bar" was published in *Between: New Gay Poetry*. Chelsea Station Editions. 2014.

"Vincent" was published on Lyrelyre.com. Gregory Crosby, Editor. 2015.

"The Carnival of Affection" was published in *Assaracus*, Vol. 16. 2015.

"Roses" was published by HIV Here & Now. Michael Broder, Editor. 2015.

# WITH THANKS

A first book has a lot of midwives (and midhusbands) who attend its nativity. There are many to thank for staying by me through its gestation. First, my publisher: Sibling Rivalry Press. Bryan Borland and my editor, Seth Pennington, have been constant friends and colleagues in this endeavor and it has meant so much to me; I am happy to have joined the family. I also wish to thank my professors, mentors and advisors at City College, New York, where many of these poems were written over the past four years: Michelle Valladeres, Geraldine Murphy, Cynthia Zarin, Elaine Sexton, Pamela Laskin, Paul Oppenheimer, and Harold Veeser.

To the poet and writer friends in my life, of which there are many who, with camaraderie and good humor, continue to inspire me and keep me on the path, I want to thank Richard Foerster, Gavin Geoffrey Dillard, Dean Kostos, Carlos Pintado, Michele Karas, Robert Carr, Kateri Lanthier, Laura Argiri, and Scott Rex Hightower, among so many more new poets who continue to keep me in their tribe. I am very grateful to each one of them. To those poets with whom I studied and created some of the poems in this volume, I thank Carl Phillips, Michael Klein, Mark Doty, Nickole Brown and Jessica Jacobs.

With great love and friendship, I salute in gratitude Scott Mullenberg for giving this book its first 'house,' and also friends Paul Pinkman and Ronaldo Aguiar for helping to make that house a visual beauty with their art.

To my family, my sisters—Barbara, Kathleen, Theresa and Stephanie—thank you for walking with me and letting me know there is more walking together ahead still to do. Kathleen, you are always on my shoulder.

And to Daniel J. Hurley, III, without whom this book would never be.

And of course, to E.D., my eternal Bride of Permanence.

*"Speech is one symptom of affection"*

—*Emily Dickinson*

# ABOUT THE PRESS

Sibling Rivalry Press is an independent press based in Little Rock, Arkansas. It is a sponsored project of Fractured Atlas, a nonprofit arts service organization. Contributions to support the operations of Sibling Rivalry Press are tax-deductible to the extent permitted by law, and your donations will directly assist in the publication of work that disturbs and enraptures. To contribute to the publication of more books like this one, please visit our website and click *donate*.

Sibling Rivalry Press gratefully acknowledges the following donors, without whom this book would not be possible:

| | | |
|---|---|---|
| TJ Acena | JP Howard | Tina Parker |
| Kaveh Akbar | Shane Khosropour | Brody Parrish Craig |
| John-Michael Albert | Randy Kitchens | Patrick Pink |
| Kazim Ali | Jørgen Lien | Dennis Rhodes |
| Seth Eli Barlow | Stein Ove Lien | Paul Romero |
| Virginia Bell | Sandy Longhorn | Robert Siek |
| Ellie Black | Ed Madden | Scott Siler |
| Laure-Anne Bosselaar | Jessica Manack | Alana Smoot Samuelson |
| Dustin Brookshire | Sam & Mark Manivong | Loria Taylor |
| Alessandro Brusa | Thomas March | Hugh Tipping |
| Jessie Carty | Telly McGaha & Justin Brown | Alex J. Tunney |
| Philip F. Clark | Donnelle McGee | Ray Warman & Dan Kiser |
| Morell E. Mullins | David Meischen | Ben Westlie |
| Jonathan Forrest | Ron Mohring | Valerie Wetlaufer |
| Hal Gonzales | Laura Mullen | Nicholas Wong |
| Diane Greene | Eric Nguyen | Anonymous (18) |
| Brock Guthrie | David A. Nilsen | |
| Chris Herrmann | Joseph Osmundson | |

# ABOUT THE POET

Philip F. Clark is an adjunct lecturer in English at City College, New York, where he received his MFA in Creative Writing in 2016. His poems have been published in *Assaracus, Lyrelyre, The Good Men Project, Poetry in Performance,* and *HIV Here & Now.* Most recently his work is included in *Transition: Poems in the Aftermath,* the new anthology of resistance poetry published by Indolent Books. His poetry reviews and interviews have been published in *Lambda Literary Review* and *The Conversant.* His poetry blog is *The Poet's Grin:*

philipfclark.wordpress.com

CPSIA information can be obtained
at www.ICGtesting.com
Printed in the USA
FFOW03n1806060618
47016337-49284FF

9 781943 977413